THE MONEY MAGNET MANTRAS

A Step-by-Step Guide to Making and Retaining Money

Mohd Faisal

Copyright © 2023 Mohd Faisal

All rights reserved

The characters and events portrayed in this book are fictitious. Any similarity to real persons, living or dead, is coincidental and not intended by the author.

No part of this book may be reproduced, or stored in a retrieval system, or transmitted in any form or by any means, electronic, mechanical, photocopying, recording, or otherwise, without express written permission of the publisher.

Dedication

To God, the Almighty,

"The Money Magnet Mantras: A Step-by-Step Guide to Making and Retaining Money," which I dedicate to You, is written with the utmost respect and thanks. All wealth, knowledge, and divine direction come from you. This effort serves as a humble witness to Your unending grace and unending gifts.

To all readers,

You, the searchers and dreamers who desire to discover the keys to material wealth and build an abundant life, are the target audience for this book. I am grateful for the opportunity to travel this path with you, and I dedicate these pages to your unshakable dedication and kind hearts.

I hope these words will help you feel inspired, clear, and empowered. May the sage advice and doable measures given in this book help you reach your financial objectives and alter your relationship with money.

Together, let's set out on this transforming journey, led by the values of abundance, appreciation, and deliberate wealth building. May this book act as a spark for good, bringing forth the hidden potential in you to become a real money magnet.

from the bottom of my heart, with love

~Mohd Faisal

"Opportunities are like magnets, attracting those who are open to receiving them."

~ANONYMOUS

CONTENTS

Title Page
Copyright
Dedication
Epigraph
Preface
Chapter 1: Introduction   1
Chapter 2: Building a Wealth Mindset   9
Chapter 3: Creating Money Mantras That Work   19
Chapter 4: Activating the Law of Attraction   28
Chapter 5: Money-Making Strategies   36
Chapter 6: The Art of Retaining Wealth   46
Chapter 7: Overcoming Financial Challenges   56
Chapter 8: Nurturing Your Money Magnet Lifestyle   66
Chapter 9: Conclusion   76
Epilogue   85
About The Author   89
Books By This Author   91
The End   97

PREFACE

"The Money Magnet Mantras: A Step-by-Step Guide to Making and Retaining Money" welcomes you!

Without a question, money plays a crucial part in our lives. It molds our possibilities and impacts our choices, as well as providing us with the resources to achieve our hopes and objectives. Whether we acknowledge it or not, we all want financial stability, yet for many, it remains an unattainable objective.

This book was developed with a single goal in mind: to provide you with the information, skills, and attitude required to become a money magnet. It is intended to take you on a transforming journey through the ideas of abundance, wealth creation, and financial intelligence.

"The Money Magnet Mantras" is not your usual quick-money program. It is not about rapid success or miracles. Instead, it emphasizes a comprehensive strategy that considers both the external and internal factors of wealth growth. It dives into the psychology of money, addressing the attitude and beliefs that may be preventing you from reaching your financial objectives.

Throughout these pages, you will find useful tactics, tried-and-true approaches, and insightful information to help you make and keep money. This book gives a thorough route to financial plenty, from understanding the fundamentals of financial literacy to mastering the art of investing, from adopting a prosperity mentality to building a tailored wealth strategy.

"The Money Magnet Mantras" provides you with a wealth of knowledge and inspiration by drawing on the wisdom of great entrepreneurs, investors, and wealth creators. It mixes ancient concepts with current methods, providing a step-by-step guide to the ever-changing financial world.

I invite you to approach this adventure with an open mind and a readiness to rethink your previous money views. Prepare to take action, to adopt new habits and attitudes, and to make the required adjustments in your life in order to attract and maintain riches.

Remember that being a money magnet is about having the abilities and attitude that will allow you to build your own riches. your book is your guide, mentor, and ally in your endeavor. It will give you the ability to take charge of your financial destiny and open the door to a life of prosperity and joy.

I am ecstatic for you and the opportunities that await you. So, let us go on this life-changing trip together. May "The Money Magnet Mantras" serve as your guide and source of inspiration as you begin on your journey to financial independence.

I wish you prosperity and success.

[Mohd Faisal]

CHAPTER 1: INTRODUCTION

Welcome To The Money Magnet Journey.

Consider a life in which money pours easily into your bank account. A life in which financial prosperity is your constant companion and prospects for wealth creation abound. Welcome to the Money Magnet Journey, a transforming journey into the power of money mantras and their potential to produce riches in your life.

This chapter lays the groundwork for your thrilling journey into the world of financial achievement. We urge you to imagine the possibilities that await you and to be open to the unlimited potential that resides inside you. Are you ready to let your inner money magnet shine?

You may be wondering what a money magnet is. Consider it a power inside yourself that attracts riches, opportunity, and success. You may shift your financial reality and build the life you've always desired by tapping into this energy.

Throughout this trip, we'll learn about money mantras, which are powerful affirmations and words that, when repeated with purpose and belief, have the capacity to reprogram your subconscious mind and align it with your financial objectives. But it's not simply repeating words; it's about adopting an abundant attitude, adjusting your viewpoint, and taking creative action.

Before we go any further, let's take a time to consider your present relationship with money. Are there any limiting thoughts or bad connections that may be preventing you from moving forward? This is a secure environment for you to explore those ideas and let go of any self-imposed limitations.

The Money Magnet Journey is not a get-rich-quick scam that promises instant wealth. It is a comprehensive wealth-creation strategy that includes mentality, activity, and alignment. We will walk you through the process step by step, giving practical tools and activities to help you make good changes and attract financial plenty.

You will discover how to establish a wealth attitude, construct individual money mantras, activate the powerful Law of Attraction, develop money-making techniques, maintain your riches via wise financial planning, and overcome hurdles as we move through this book. We will provide you with the information, insights, and strategies you need to succeed in the arena of wealth.

We urge you to embark on this path with an open heart and an open mind to change. Remember that you have the power to rewrite your financial narrative and build an abundant future. The road isn't always easy, but with perseverance, persistence, and a dash of magic, you can become a genuine money magnet.

So take a deep breath and prepare to go on an unbelievable adventure. We're happy to have you join us on this life-changing journey to financial freedom. Prepare to reveal the secrets, harness your inner strength, and go on the Money Magnet Journey.

Understanding The Power Of Money Mantras

Consider this: You awaken in the morning with a burst of drive and energy. As you get ready for the day, you say a sequence of motivating mantras that instill in you a feeling of plenty and financial well-being. These sentences, known as money mantras, have the capacity to shift your relationship with money and open up a world of financial prospects.

Money mantras are simple but powerful affirmations meant to retrain your subconscious mind and connect your ideas, beliefs, and actions with the wealth you want. They serve as a link between your conscious goals and the universal spirit of success, allowing you to generate and keep money with ease.

Money mantras have the capacity to alter your thinking from scarcity to abundance. For far too long, society has conditioned us to believe in financial restrictions and scarcity. We've been bombarded with messages telling us that money is scarce, that there isn't enough to go around, and that we must fight and sacrifice in order to attain financial success. These ideas become self-fulfilling, locking us in a cycle of scarcity and constraint.

Money mantras stop the loop by teaching new, powerful money attitudes. They upend the existing quo and remind us that abundance is our natural state. We begin to reprogram our subconscious mind by repeating these positive affirmations on a daily basis, replacing old, limiting ideas with new, expanded ones. We begin to adjust our energy frequency and attract money chances and wealth.

Money mantras, on the other hand, are not a mystical incantation that instantaneously creates money in your life. They collaborate with your ideas, emotions, and behaviors. When you repeat money mantras, you are sending a strong message to the universe that you are prepared for and deserve financial wealth. However, it is critical to back up these slogans with consistent action. Be open and aggressive in pursuing and grasping possibilities that lead to financial success while you repeat your mantras. Your mantras serve as a spark for inspired activity, and the universe reacts to inspired action.

When it comes to harnessing the power of money mantras, consistency is essential. Include them in your everyday routine by including them into your morning or evening routines. Accept them as financial affirmations and repeat them with conviction and confidence. The more you embrace your mantras' energy, the more they get imprinted in your subconscious mind, impacting your ideas, choices, and, eventually, your financial reality.

Money mantras should not be used in place of financial knowledge, strategic planning, or hard effort. They are a complimentary tool that helps you improve your thinking and take inspired action toward your financial objectives. When you combine the power of money mantras with realistic financial methods, continual learning, and focused work, you'll discover a powerful recipe for creating and keeping money.

Money mantras provide a refuge of optimism and possibilities in a world where money may be a cause of worry and anxiety. They remind us that we have the capacity to change our connection with money and that we are co-creators of our financial future. So, harness the power of money mantras, allow them to lead you to financial success, and watch as the world conspires to offer you the prosperity you deserve.

Setting Your Financial Intentions:

Imagine beginning on a trip with no clear objective in mind. It's the equivalent of setting sail without a compass or map, leaving your destiny to chance. The same may be said for your financial path. You risk wandering aimlessly and losing out on the richness that awaits you if you do not establish clear objectives for financial success.

Intentions work as potent guideposts, guiding your attention, energy, and actions toward the achievement of your goals. Setting financial intentions becomes much more important. It all comes down to matching your ideas, beliefs, and actions with the wealth you want to generate and keep.

So, how can you establish financial success intentions? It all starts with a thorough examination of your financial goals and a real desire to change your relationship with money. It's about transitioning from a scarcity attitude to an abundance mindset, from uncertainty to firm faith in your potential to attain financial wealth.

Begin by making time to think on what financial success genuinely means to you. Is it about retiring comfortably, touring the globe, providing for your family, or making a difference via philanthropy? Your intentions should be very personal and significant to you, and should be based on your beliefs and goals.

It is critical to picture the future you want when you establish your aspirations. Close your eyes and clearly visualize yourself having a prosperous life. Consider yourself surrounded by success symbols such as financial stability, a lovely house, satisfying experiences, and the flexibility to follow your interests. Allow yourself to experience the thrill, joy, and thankfulness that comes with having met your financial objectives.

Once you've established a clear vision of your ideal financial future, it's crucial to express your aspirations in positive, motivating language. Use affirmations and statements that speak to you and make you feel hopeful. For example, "I am a magnet for wealth and abundance," "I attract lucrative opportunities effortlessly," or "I am financially free and prosperous."

Remember that aspirations are more than just wishful thinking; they need action and dedication. Your ambitions should be matched with a plan—a step-by-step guide to making your dreams a reality. Break down your financial objectives into smaller, more manageable stages, and identify the exact measures you will take to bring your plans to fruition. Investing in your education, establishing a company, or saving a particular proportion of your salary all contribute to your financial success.

Consider making visual reminders to reinforce your aims. Put your aspirations on sticky notes and post them wherever you'll see them every day, like your bathroom mirror, computer screen, or wallet. Use visualization methods on a daily basis to strengthen the emotional link between your objectives and your actions. Make a vision board with pictures that symbolize your financial objectives, and spend a few minutes each day immersing yourself in the sensations of having already accomplished them.

Setting financial success goals is a continual effort. As you travel, examine and revise your objectives on a frequent basis. Celebrate your accomplishments along the road and change your route as appropriate. Maintain an open mind to new prospects and be prepared to adjust your plans when circumstances change. When your goals are clear, concentrated, and connected with your greatest good, the world will conspire to help you create your financial ambitions.

Setting your aspirations for financial success puts you in control of your financial path. You take an active role in manifesting the prosperity and plenty you seek. Set your objectives boldly, with passion and purpose, and watch as the world aligns itself to bring you closer to your financial goals. You have the ability to attract and keep money, and it all begins with a clear goal.

CHAPTER 2: BUILDING A WEALTH MINDSET

Developing An Abundance Mindset.

Consider seeing the world through an abundance lens—one that sees boundless chances and possibilities, as well as an unyielding confidence that there is more than enough for everyone, including yourself. When it comes to money, this is the core of establishing an abundant attitude.

An abundance mentality is a way of thinking that acknowledges and welcomes the concept that we have an abundance of resources, riches, and possibilities. It is the polar opposite of a scarcity mindset, which is based on fear, poverty, and the conviction that there is a limited quantity of riches available.

Cultivating an abundant mindset is essential for financial success because it influences how you view and interact with money. When you work from an abundant mentality, you open yourself up to a world of possibilities and easily attract riches. It becomes a self-fulfilling prophesy when your ideas, beliefs, and actions connect with the abundant energy, resulting in financial development and wealth.

So, how can you develop an abundant mindset when it comes to money? It all starts with adjusting your thinking and emphasis from scarcity to abundance. Here are some essential first steps:

Recognize your present financial thinking and beliefs.

Do you often worry about not having enough? Do you compare yourself to others and feel inadequate? The first step in breaking away from a scarcity mindset is awareness.

Gratitude:

Give thanks for what you already have. Gratitude redirects your attention from what you lack to what you value, allowing you to see the wealth that already exists in your life. Spend some time each day expressing thankfulness for your financial gifts, no matter how little they may seem.

Affirmations for an abundant attitude:

Use affirmations to reprogram your subconscious mind and

strengthen your abundant attitude. Affirmations assist to reprogram your thoughts and promote a good connection with money. For example, "I am a magnet for wealth and abundance," "Money flows to me effortlessly," or "I attract limitless opportunities for financial success."

Abundant Mentors and Role Models:

Surround yourself with people who have an abundant mindset. Seek for financial success mentors or role models and learn from their thinking and tactics. Their thinking will impact and inspire yours.

Focus on Possibilities:

Train your mind to recognize possibilities and opportunities rather than limits. Instead of focusing on what may go wrong, consider what could go well. Make it a habit to explore for answers and new opportunities for financial progress.

Generosity:

Perform generous and charitable deeds. Accept the idea that there is plenty for everyone and share your resources. This abundant attitude generates a flow of energy and invites more wealth into your life.

Invest in your financial education and personal growth via continuous learning. Increase your understanding of money management, investing, and wealth generation. The more you understand, the more confident you will be in making sound financial choices.

Remember that establishing an abundant mindset is a continuous process. It takes time, perseverance, and a dedication to confronting and modifying your money views. Mind your thoughts, choose abundance over scarcity, and surround yourself with good influencers that support your perspective.

You will notice a significant difference in your connection with money as you create an abundant mindset. You'll become a magnet for financial possibilities, more easily attract riches, and face obstacles with a resilient and hopeful outlook. Accept the power of plenty and watch as your financial situation changes before your eyes.

Overcoming Money Limiting Beliefs:

Consider yourself bound by invisible shackles that limit your financial progress and keep you from attaining your full potential. These shackles are your limiting views about money—deeply established attitudes and perceptions that impede your financial success. It's time to break free from these shackles and reinvent your financial narrative.

Money-limiting ideas are often acquired early in life, affected by our upbringing, cultural training, and previous experiences. They mold our money-related ideas, feelings, and actions, preventing us from accepting the richness that is accessible to us.

The good news is that you have the ability to transcend these limiting assumptions and establish a new financial story. Here are some important actions to help you break free:

Begin by recognizing and admitting your limiting assumptions about money. Consider the messages you learned about money as a child, as well as any bad experiences or ideas you still have. The first step toward change is being aware.

Question Your Beliefs:

Call into question the veracity of your limiting beliefs. Consider if your opinions are founded on facts or assumptions. Are they assisting me or hindering my progress? Replace self-limiting ideas with ones that empower you. Change "Money is the root of all evil" to "Money is a powerful tool that can create positive change in my life and the lives of others."

Reinterpret Past Experiences:

Examine your previous financial experiences and reinterpret them in a favorable perspective. Instead of seeing financial losses as failures, consider them great learning experiences that have built your resilience and resourcefulness.

Seek powerful proof:

Look for proof that backs up your new, powerful money views. Surround yourself with success stories, read books written by people who have attained financial plenty, and network with others who have a good attitude about money. This will assist to cement your new views while also laying a solid basis for your financial progress.

Affirmations:

Affirmations may be used to remodel your subconscious mind. Repeat positive words like "I am worthy of financial abundance," "Money flows to me easily and effortlessly," or "I deserve to be financially successful." By continuously repeating good ideas, you may replace limiting beliefs with powerful ones.

Visualization:

Imagine yourself having a prosperous life. Create vivid mental pictures of yourself reaching your financial objectives, having financial independence, and living the life you want. Use your senses and experience the feelings linked with your vision. Visualization aids in the rewiring of your brain and the alignment of your subconscious mind with your chosen reality.

Take Inspired Action:

Take inspired action toward your financial objectives to break away from the paralysis created by limiting ideas. Begin modest and progressively expand your activities. Every action you take strengthens your idea that you are capable of generating financial prosperity.

Surround Yourself with People Who Are optimistic About Money:

Surround yourself with people who are optimistic about money.

Join groups or look for mentors who can provide direction, support, and inspiration as you work to overcome limiting beliefs.

Remember that eliminating limiting ideas about money takes time, self-compassion, and constant work. Be kind to yourself as you embark on this changing adventure. Celebrate your accomplishments, no matter how modest, and believe that each step forward will bring you closer to financial freedom.

By testing and conquering your limiting views about money, you make room in your life for new possibilities and opportunities. Accept the powerful conviction that you are worthy of and capable of financial achievement. Rewrite your money narrative and watch as your fresh beliefs build an abundant and prosperous future.

Developing A Positive Relationship With Money:

Consider riches to be a close friend who encourages and uplifts you while offering the resources to live a full and abundant life. It's time to have a healthy relationship with riches and welcome it into your life. You may create a peaceful and powerful relationship with riches by adjusting your mentality and attitudes toward wealth.

Release Negative Associations:

Begin by releasing any negative associations or judgements you have about riches. Recognize that money is neither good nor evil in and of itself; rather, it is a tool that can be utilized to produce positive effects and possibilities. Remove any feelings of guilt or shame you may have about wanting financial plenty.

Redefine Wealth:

Think about wealth in terms other than monetary worth. Wealth includes not just financial assets but also health, relationships, personal development, and experiences. You may understand the holistic nature of riches and live a well-rounded and meaningful life by extending your viewpoint.

Adopt an Abundance Mindset:

Adopt an abundance mindset in which you feel there is more than enough riches to go around. Abundance is not a finite resource, but rather a limitless reservoir of possibilities. Accept the notion that by creating riches, you are positively contributing to the world, therefore helping yourself and others.

Align with Your principles:

Make certain that your quest of riches is consistent with your basic principles. Define wealth for yourself and how it may be utilized to make a good difference in your life and the lives of others. When your money matches your ideals, it becomes a strong force for good.

Gratitude & Appreciation:

Make a practice of thanking God for the prosperity and richness you already have. Gratitude focuses your attention away from what is missing and onto what is there, developing a healthy connection with riches. Recognize and appreciate the possibilities, resources, and blessings that are presented to you.

Money as a Tool:

Consider money to be a tool that allows you to live the life you want and make a difference in the world. Accept money as a tool for expressing your beliefs, supporting causes you care about, and investing in your personal and professional development. Consider money to be a companion on your trip rather than an aim in itself.

Share and Give:

Recognize and appreciate the power of generosity and giving. When you have an excess of riches, spread it around by performing acts of kindness, generosity, or supporting causes that are important to you. Giving promotes a good energy flow and strengthens your positive connection with riches.

Invest in your financial education and personal development to ensure continuous learning and growth. Develop information and skills that will enable you to make educated financial choices and manage riches responsibly. Keep an open mind when it comes to learning from experts, mentors, and successful people who can inspire and lead you on your path.

You may build an atmosphere of plenty, success, and well-being by establishing a good relationship with money. Because your thinking and attitudes affect your financial reality, pick ideas and beliefs that promote your financial success and satisfaction. Accept money as a strong ally, connect it with your beliefs, and use it as a catalyst for living an abundant life and having a great effect on the world.

CHAPTER 3: CREATING MONEY MANTRAS THAT WORK

Making Your Own Money Affirmations.

Personalizing money affirmations is an effective technique to retrain your subconscious mind and connect your ideas, beliefs, and actions with the financial prosperity you seek. You may increase the impact of affirmations and make them more significant to your journey by personalizing them to your unique objectives and ambitions. Here's how to make customised money affirmations step by step:

Identify Your Financial Objectives:

Begin by defining your financial objectives. What financial goals do you have? Is it a certain quantity of money saved, the commencement of a successful company, the purchase of real estate, or the elimination of debt? Determine what you want to see in your financial life.

Concentrate on Empowering Beliefs:

Consider the beliefs and mentality you wish to create in regard to your financial objectives. Consider the following beliefs: plenty, prosperity, financial liberty, success, and confidence. Choose powerful beliefs that will help you achieve your objectives.

Use Positive Language:

Use positive language to frame your affirmations. Instead of concentrating on what you don't want or what you don't have, concentrate on what you do want to attract and create. Change "I don't want to be in debt" to "I am debt-free and financially secure."

Make Them Personal and Present Tense:

Write your affirmations in the present tense, as if you have already attained your desired financial situation. Use personal pronouns like "I" or "my" to personalize and affect them. Say, for example, "I am a successful entrepreneur" rather than "I will become a successful entrepreneur."

Keep Affirmations Brief and precise:

Keep your affirmations brief and precise. This aids in concentration and amplifies the intended consequence. Instead of a long affirmation, make a brief yet forceful remark. For instance, "I attract abundance in all areas of my life" or "I am open to receiving unlimited financial opportunities."

Incorporate Emotion and imagery:

Incorporate emotion and imagery into your affirmations. As you repeat the affirmations, feel the feelings involved with reaching your financial objectives. Imagine yourself already living your ideal financial reality, feeling pleasure, freedom, and achievement.

Repeat Frequently and Consistently:

Make a commitment to repeating your specific money affirmations on a regular and consistent basis. Set aside time each day to say your affirmations, either in the morning or before going to bed. Repetition strengthens good attitudes and aids in the reprogramming of your subconscious mind.

Believe and Act As If:

Believe in the truth and power of your affirmations as you say them. Embody the enthusiasm of having previously met your financial objectives. Allow your affirmations to inspire and drive you to take action in the direction of your objectives. Act as though you already have the financial plenty you seek.

Remember that tailored money affirmations work best when they are linked with your own aspirations, beliefs, and values. They can help you rewire your attitude and empower yourself on your financial path. Accept them with conviction, repetition, and consistency, and watch as they produce good improvements in your money relationship and your financial well-being.

Increasing The Power Of Your Mantras:

Amplifying the energy of your mantras is an important exercise that may help you connect with the affirmations more deeply and increase their manifestation power. You may speed up the process of attracting and manifesting your desired financial results by infusing your mantras with purpose, passion, and concentrated energy. Here are some ways to boost the power of your mantras:

Find or construct a calm, tranquil location where you may practice your mantras without interruptions. This place might be a single room, a corner of your house, or even an outdoor area. Make it relaxing and favorable to introspection and inner work.

Set Clear Intentions:

Before you start repeating your mantras, make a list of what you wish to materialize. Visualize your financial objectives, experience the emotions connected with reaching them, and instill clarity and purpose in your plans. This assists in aligning your energies and focusing your attention.

Deep Breathing and Relaxation:

Take a few seconds to quiet your mind and body by engaging in deep breathing and relaxation techniques. Deep breathing aids in the oxygenation of your cells, the relaxation of your nervous system, and the creation of a receptive condition for absorbing good affirmations.

Recite your mantras with conviction:

Recite your mantras with conviction and believe in their reality. Speak them loudly or quietly, but fill them with powerful and unyielding energy. Feel the power of each phrase as you confirm it, knowing that it is bringing your thoughts into alignment and attracting the ideal financial consequences.

Emotion and Visualization: As you repeat your mantras, engage your emotions and imagine the fulfillment of your financial objectives. Feel the delight, excitement, and thankfulness that comes with having already accomplished those objectives. Imagine yourself enjoying the rich life you wish, and let that energy to pervade your whole body.

Incorporate Physical Movement:

To amp up the energy, incorporate physical movement into your mantra practice. Gentle stretching, yoga poses, or even dance may be included. Movement assists in the activation of your body's energy centers, known as chakras, and generates a harmonious flow of energy throughout your existence.

Use Props and Visual Aids:

Incorporate props or visual aids that symbolize your financial objectives into your mantra practice. This might contain photographs of your ideal home, vision boards with images of your ideal lifestyle, or artifacts that represent richness and success. These visual clues act as reminders and help to ground the energy of your chants.

appreciation and Release:

Finish your mantra practice by expressing appreciation for your financial objectives coming true. Let go of any connection to the result and believe that the universe is on your side. Allow any doubts or anxieties to fade and submit to the flow of riches.

Aligning Your Mantras With Your Financial Objectives:

Aligning your mantras with your financial objectives is critical for maximizing the power of positive affirmations and generating the desired financial results. When your mantras align with your objectives, beliefs, and aspirations, they provide a focused and deliberate energy that drives you to financial success. Here are some strategies to help you match your mantras with your financial objectives:

Clarify Your Financial objectives:

Begin by defining your precise financial objectives. Make your writing as precise and thorough as possible. For example, if you want to make a certain amount of money, specify how much you want to earn and when you want to do it. Make a list of your objectives in a clear and straightforward way.

Identify any limiting ideas or negative thinking patterns that may be preventing you from reaching your financial objectives. These beliefs might be impediments to your success. Common limiting thoughts about money include "money is scarce," "I am undeserving of wealth," and "I am not capable of earning a lot of money." Recognize these beliefs and be prepared to dispute and replace them with positive, empowering attitudes.

Create Affirmations:

Create unique affirmations that specifically target your financial objectives and the limiting beliefs you wish to overcome. Create affirmations that represent the good result you wish to achieve as well as the powerful ideas you want to embrace. If you want to establish a profitable company, for example, your affirmation may be "I am a successful and prosperous business owner, attracting abundance and opportunities."

Make Them current Tense and Positive:

Make your affirmations current tense and positive. This creates a feeling of urgency and promotes the impression that your objectives are already being realized. For example, rather of stating, "I will achieve financial freedom," say, "I am financially free and abundant."

Accept Visualization:

Include visualization in your mantra practice. Visualize yourself actually living your financial objectives while you speak your affirmations. Create vivid mental imagery of what it looks, feels, and sounds like to have met your financial goals. Engage all of your senses and immerse yourself in the success and riches sensation.

Repeat Consistently:

When it comes to matching your mantras with your financial objectives, consistency is essential. Affirmations should be repeated at least once a day. Set out a certain time and place for your mantra practice and make it a non-negotiable component of your daily routine. Repetition increases the brain circuits linked with your objectives and supports your conviction in your ability to achieve them.

Believe and Act As If:

As you repeat your mantras, fully believe in their power and reality. Embody the enthusiasm of having previously met your financial objectives. Allow your affirmations to inspire and drive you to take action in the direction of your objectives. Act as though you already have the financial plenty you seek. This connection of thought and behavior speeds up the manifestation process.

Update and Evolve:

As your financial objectives change, assess and update your mantras on a regular basis. As you develop or new chances present themselves, modify your affirmations to suit your current goals and beliefs. Your mantras should constantly correspond to your current aspirations and intentions.

You may establish a strong synergy between your ideas, beliefs, and actions by matching your mantras with your financial objectives. This alignment creates the conditions for you to materialize your desired financial results and bring prosperity into your life. Maintain your commitment, attention, and faith in the process.

Your synchronized mantras will assist you in staying on track and manifesting the financial success you seek.

CHAPTER 4: ACTIVATING THE LAW OF ATTRACTION

Using Visualization To Your Advantage.

Using visualization to speed the manifestation of your financial objectives is a powerful skill. You engage your subconscious mind and link your energy with the universe's unlimited possibilities by vividly picturing and experiencing your desired results. Here's how to use visualization to your advantage:

Create a Clear Vision:

Begin by developing a thorough vision of your financial objectives. Visualize your desired outcome, whether it's a precise salary, financial independence, or a great company. Visualize the specifics, such as the figures in your bank account, the lifestyle you want, or the effect you want to create with your riches.

Engage Your Senses:

Visualization is most successful when all of your senses are engaged. Immerse yourself in the experience as you picture your financial achievement. Visualize your chosen reality's colors, forms, and textures. Listen for the noises linked with your financial success. Experience delight, excitement, and contentment. The more intensely your senses are engaged, the more real and palpable your image becomes.

Incorporate Emotion:

Emotion gives your visualization exercise more strength and depth. Feel the good feelings that come with attaining your financial objectives. Profitable people have a feeling of wealth, thankfulness, and contentment. Allow your emotions to flow through your body, infusing energy and passion into your visualization practice.

Visualization Ritual:

As part of your everyday practice, develop a consistent visualization ritual. Set aside time every day to imagine your financial objectives. Find a quiet, comfortable place where you can rest and concentrate. To improve the experience, combine visualization with meditation, deep breathing exercises, or relaxing background music.

Consistent practice is essential for harnessing the power of visualization. Make visualizing your financial objectives a regular habit. Consistency creates momentum and increases your faith in the potential of your vision. Even a few minutes each day might add up to a big impact over time.

Be Specific and practical:

While large dreams are important, make sure your visions are specific and practical. Divide your objectives into smaller milestones and picture each step along the way. This allows you to retain clarity and concentration, making your idea more accessible and credible.

Picture possible barriers and Solutions:

It is also critical to picture any possible barriers or problems that may come on your financial path. Visualize yourself conquering these challenges with confidence and tenacity. Visualize the answers and methods you will use to overcome any obstacles. You strengthen your determination and boost your chances of success by mentally preparing for problems.

Take Inspired Action:

Visualization isn't enough on its own; it has to be followed with inspired action. Use your visualization practice to provide inspiration and advice while you take action toward your objectives. Allow your visions to spark new ideas and methods for your everyday life. Take steady, meaningful movements toward your goal.

Remember that visualization is a strong tool that must be used in conjunction with belief, intention, and action. As you use visualization to your advantage, believe in the process and stay open to receiving possibilities and synchronicities that will help you on your financial path. Your vividly envisioned visions will aid in the manifestation of your financial objectives and pave the way to the affluent life you seek.

Gratitude Practice For Financial Abundance:

Practicing appreciation for financial wealth may change your thinking, bring more riches into your life, and enhance your feeling of joy. By concentrating on what you currently have and expressing gratitude for your financial benefits, you build a strong energy that attracts even more riches. Here's how to cultivate financial abundance gratitude:

Count Your benefits:

Begin by establishing a list of all of your present financial benefits and abundance. A solid salary, a pleasant house, supportive relationships, or any other financial resources that provide you pleasure and security are examples of this. Recognize and appreciate every item on your list.

Gratitude Journaling:

Set aside time each day to write down your financial blessings. Write down particular items for which you are thankful, such as unexpected money windfalls, profitable investments, job prospects, or the capacity to meet your wants and goals. Consider the effect these benefits have had on your life.

Instead of obsessing on what you lack or what you want to accomplish financially, change your emphasis to the wealth that currently exists in your life. Train your mind to recognize the possibilities, resources, and blessings that are all around you. This adjustment in viewpoint allows greater riches to enter your life.

Make it a habit to show thanks for your financial plenty on a daily basis. This may be accomplished by the use of affirmations, prayers, or just speaking out. Thank God for the money you make, the possibilities that come your way, and your financial security. The energy of thankfulness is amplified when it is expressed verbally.

Awareness Practice:

Incorporate awareness into your financial experiences. Bring awareness to the wealth that is pouring in and out of your life when you spend money, pay bills, or participate in financial activities. Be totally present in these times and practice thankfulness for the money flow that keeps you going.

Share and Give Back:

Develop a generous heart by sharing your financial prosperity with others. Give to causes or people who are less fortunate. Generosity not only helps others, but it also increases your appreciation for what you have. Giving creates a positive circle of plenty and expands your ability to accept more.

Appreciation Visualization:

Include appreciation for financial wealth in your visualization exercise. Think of yourself as being surrounded by money, success, and prosperity. Feel grateful in your heart for all of your financial gifts. Consider how you may give and receive with an open and appreciative heart.

Maintain a thanksgiving practice:

Create a daily or weekly thanksgiving practice focused on your financial wealth. This might include lighting a candle, praying, or reflecting on thankfulness. Consistency in your practice promotes the spirit of appreciation while also keeping you in line with the flow of financial plenty.

By practicing gratitude for financial plenty on a daily basis, you alter your thinking from scarcity to abundance, attract additional possibilities, and increase your appreciation for life's rewards. This technique generates a pleasant vibe that attracts more success and satisfaction. Accept appreciation as a strong tool in your financial path and see how it changes your relationship with money.

Using Mantras To Attract Opportunities And Wealth:

Throughout numerous spiritual traditions, mantras have been employed to conjure good energy, attract riches, and manifest money. Incorporating mantras from other belief systems may create a unique and potent way to attracting chances and prosperity. Here are six mantras or prayers from various traditions:

"Om Shreem Maha Lakshmiyei Namaha"
is a Sanskrit Vedic Mantra.
This mantra is dedicated to Lakshmi, the Hindu goddess of riches and plenty. Chanting this mantra requests Goddess Lakshmi's blessings to promote financial riches and chances.

"La Ilaha Illa Allah"

is a Sufi mantra.

This powerful Islamic mantra translates to "There is no god but Allah." It serves as a reminder of the ultimate source of all plenty and begs heavenly blessings for attracting money and chances.

"Rabbana atina fid-dunya hasanatan wa fil 'akhirati hasanatan waqina 'adhaban-nar"

is an Islamic Ayat.

This ayat from the Quran is a petition that translates to "Our Lord, grant us good in this world and good in the Hereafter, and save us from the punishment of the Hellfire." It asks for blessings for success, prosperity, and financial security.

"The Lord is my shepherd; I shall not want."
This Bible line from the 23rd Psalm expresses faith in God's lead-

ership and sustenance. It accepts that there will be no shortage or desire with God as the provider, inviting riches and possibilities.

"Om Mani Padme Hum"

is a Buddhist prayer.

This well-known Buddhist chant is linked with Avalokiteshvara, the bodhisattva of compassion. Chanting this mantra brings about compassion, knowledge, and good energy, all of which may attract riches and opportunity.

"Thank you for the abundance that flows into my life; I am open to receiving all opportunities for growth and prosperity,"

says the Universal Prayer.

This global prayer expresses thankfulness for the plenty that already exists and establishes the goal to be open to receiving greater possibilities and fortune. It reinforces a good outlook and brings wealth into one's life.

When employing mantras or prayers, remember to have trust, sincerity, and a clear objective. Choose the mantras that have the greatest meaning for you and integrate them into your everyday practice. Recite them with respect, concentration, and faith in their ability to bring opportunities and fortune. Consistent and committed practice of these mantras may assist in aligning your energy with wealth and causing a positive change in your financial path.

CHAPTER 5: MONEY-MAKING STRATEGIES

Investigating Income-Generating Opportunities.

There are several chances to earn money and financial prosperity in today's dynamic environment. Exploring income-generating initiatives may open up new possibilities of wealth creation, whether you're looking to supplement your existing income, establish a side company, or go on a full-time entrepreneurial adventure. Here are some important steps to assist you manage this wonderful adventure:

Identify Your Passions and talents:

Begin by reflecting on your hobbies, passions, and talents. What hobbies or industries pique your interest? What do you excel at or love doing naturally? Identifying your interests and abilities will lead you to income-generating activities that complement your strengths and provide you with satisfaction.

industry Trends and Opportunities:

Keep up to date on current industry trends and new opportunities. Conduct extensive study to find companies or sectors that are growing and have the potential to be profitable. Look for market gaps or places where you may provide a unique idea or solution.

Income Streams:

Consider different income streams and diversifying your money sources. Freelance employment, consulting, selling items or services online, investing in real estate or stocks, producing and selling digital products, or launching a small company are all examples of this. Consider numerous sources of income and think imaginatively.

Assess the Risk and possible Return:

For each income-generating business you explore, assess the risk and possible return. Consider the financial investment necessary, the time commitment required, market demand, and competition. Risk and reward must be balanced in order to make educated choices and maximize your chances of success.

Create a company Plan:

If you decide to start a company, create a detailed business plan. Provide an overview of your vision, goal, target audience, marketing plans, financial estimates, and operational data. A well-crafted business plan acts as a road map and keeps you focused on your objectives as you begin to generate cash.

Acquire Relevant information and Skills:

Arm yourself with the information and skills need to succeed in your chosen endeavor. Taking classes, attending seminars, reading books, or seeking mentoring from professionals in your industry may be part of this. Continuous learning and personal growth are essential for keeping ahead in today's competitive work environment.

Create a Professional Network:

Develop a strong professional network to assist and advise you on your income-generating path. Connect with others who share your interests, attend business events, join professional organisations, and use internet platforms and social media to broaden your network. Collaboration with others may result in beneficial alliances, mentoring opportunities, and access to new markets.

Take Careful Action:

Finally, success in revenue generating necessitates taking action. Set specific objectives and divide them down into manageable chunks. In order to put your goals into action, you must be proactive, persistent, and adaptive. Accept problems as learning opportunities and be open to alter your tactics as you gain market feedback and insights.

Monitor and assess Progress:

Track and assess the progress of your income-generating projects on a regular basis. Assess critical data, assess customer or client input, and make appropriate modifications to enhance performance. Measure your performance on a regular basis and look for methods to improve your revenue sources.

Embrace a Growth attitude:

Throughout your income-generating path, cultivate a growth attitude. Accept failure as a stepping stone to progress, have a good attitude, and remain focused on your objectives. Learn from your mistakes, adjust to changes, and appreciate your accomplishments along the road.

Exploring income-generating ideas involves a blend of enthusiasm, smart thought, and action. You may begin on a joyful and lucrative road to financial plenty with careful preparation, a desire to learn, and a proactive attitude. Remember that each enterprise represents a unique chance to develop and prosper, so embrace the process and reap the benefits of your work.

Making The Most Of Your Skills And Talents:

Your abilities and talents are one-of-a-kind gifts that may serve as the basis for earning money and achieving financial success. You may uncover possibilities and enhance your potential for money creation by identifying and using your strengths.

Here's how you can make the most of your abilities and skills:

Identify Your main Strengths:

Spend some time identifying your main strengths and abilities. Consider what you are good at and what comes easily to you. Take into account your professional abilities, personal interests, and hobbies. Understanding your abilities is the first step toward successfully exploiting them.

identify Your specialty:

After determining your strengths, restrict your focus and identify your specialty. Determine the exact area in which you can bring the greatest value and differentiate yourself from the competitors. You may present yourself as an expert and attract clients or consumers who value your unique abilities by concentrating in a certain specialty.

Understand Market Demand:

Conduct market research and analysis for your abilities and talents. Determine which industries or areas need your knowledge. Look for market gaps or places where your abilities may fill particular requirements or solve difficulties. Understanding market demand enables you to adjust your offers and optimize your earnings potential.

Create a Strong Personal Brand:

Put time and effort into creating a strong personal brand that highlights your abilities and talents. Create a distinctive professional identity that is in line with your specialty and appeals to your target audience. Create a professional website, update your social media sites, and compile a portfolio that showcases your accomplishments and talents.

Build a strong network of contacts within your business or area of expertise to network and collaborate. Attend networking events, join professional organisations, and interact with others who share your interests. Collaboration with those who have complimentary abilities might lead to new chances and broaden your horizons.

Provide Value and Solve Problems:

Concentrate on providing value and resolving issues for your clients or consumers. Recognize their pain spots, issues, and requirements, then design your services or goods to meet those demands. By regularly providing value, you establish a reputation as a trustworthy and dependable expert, which may lead to higher demand for your abilities and talents.

Continuously Improve Your Skills:

You should never stop learning and progressing. Invest in your personal and professional development by learning new skills, keeping up with industry trends, and looking for possibilities for advancement. This ongoing development guarantees that your abilities stay current and in demand in an ever-changing market.

Seek and Refine input:

Actively seek input from clients, consumers, and mentors to better understand how you may improve your abilities and offers. Accept constructive criticism as a chance to grow and enhance your work. You may continually improve your strategy and achieve even greater outcomes by integrating feedback.

Adopt an Entrepreneurial attitude:

Develop an entrepreneurial attitude that values creativity, perseverance, and a willingness to take measured risks. Be proactive in your search for new possibilities, diversifying your revenue sources, and reacting to shifting market circumstances. An entrepreneurial attitude enables you to maximize the effect of your abilities and talents.

Effectively Market Yourself:

Create effective marketing methods to showcase your abilities and talents. Make use of social media channels, generate compelling material, and capitalize on word-of-mouth referrals. Demonstrate your knowledge using case studies, testimonials, or success stories that emphasize the outcomes you've accomplished for your clients or consumers.

Remember that maximizing your skills and abilities is a continual process. As you obtain additional experience and feedback, continue to assess and adjust your strategy. You may harness your particular strengths to produce financial success and satisfaction with persistence, smart thinking, and a commitment to personal improvement.

Implementing Profitable Money-Making Strategies:

To create money and achieve financial success in today's competitive environment, it's critical to take a proactive approach. Here are some money-making strategies that can help you grow your income and generate wealth:

Identify Your Unique abilities and Areas of Interest:

Begin by recognizing your unique abilities and areas of interest. Determine your interests and areas of strength. This self-awareness will assist you in capitalizing on your abilities and pursuing money-making chances that correspond with your interests.

Consider Freelancing and Consulting:

Consider working as a freelancer or consultant and giving your talents and knowledge. Many firms are ready to pay on a project basis for specialized services. Platforms such as Upwork, Freelancer, and Fiverr allow you to connect with customers looking for certain talents and services.

Start an Online Business:

There are several prospects for entrepreneurship on the internet. Starting an internet company enables you to access a worldwide audience while maintaining minimal overhead expenses. The internet world gives a platform for success, whether it's selling items, providing services, or generating digital content.

Invest in the Stock Market:

Learn about stock investing and investigate the stock market's ability to create money. To make educated investing selections, do extensive research, remain current on market trends, and consider engaging with a financial counselor. Long-term investments may pay dividends, increase in value, and generate passive income.

Investigate the Gig Economy:

The gig economy has grown significantly in recent years. Platforms such as Uber, Airbnb, TaskRabbit, and DoorDash enable people to make money by providing transportation, renting out houses, doing jobs, or delivering things. Use these platforms to make the most of your time and resources.

Create and Monetize material:

Consider monetizing your material if you have a flair for writing, making videos, or producing podcasts. Content makers may earn money via ad income, sponsorships, subscriptions, and contributions on platforms such as YouTube, Twitch, and Patreon. To attract an audience, develop a specialty and deliver good material.

Provide Coaching or Mentoring Services:

If you have knowledge in a certain profession or business, think about providing coaching or mentoring services. People are eager to pay for experienced specialists' counsel and recommendations. Share your expertise, provide unique insights, and assist others in reaching their objectives.

Invest in Real Estate:

Real estate may be a profitable investment. Investigate investing prospects in rental properties, commercial spaces, or real estate investment trusts (REITs). Rental income and property appreciation may provide a consistent source of income over time.

Find methods to Monetize Your Hobbies and Talents:

If you have a pastime or skill that you like, look for methods to make money from it. There may be possibilities to sell your products, provide lessons, or perform at events if you like photography, painting, creating, or playing a musical instrument.

Create Multiple revenue Streams:

Diversify your revenue streams to decrease risk and boost earning possibilities. It is dangerous to rely exclusively on one source of income. To generate several sources of income, consider part-time work, investments, royalties, or affiliate marketing.

Remember that financial success involves hard work, persistence, and ongoing education. Maintain current knowledge of industry trends, embrace new technology and opportunities, and be ready to adapt to changing market dynamics. Implementing these excellent money-making strategies, in conjunction with hard work and commitment, may pave the road for financial prosperity and satisfaction.

CHAPTER 6: THE ART OF RETAINING WEALTH

Budgeting And Financial Planning.

B udgeting and financial planning are critical components of good money management. They serve as a road map for accomplishing your financial objectives and assisting you in making sound choices about spending, saving, and investing. Let's look at the significance of financial planning and budgeting, as well as some crucial tactics to consider.

Understanding Your Financial Objectives:

Begin by outlining your short-term and long-term financial objectives. Whether you're looking to purchase a home, save for retirement, pay off debt, or start a company, clearly defining your goals gives you a feeling of direction and purpose.

Taking Stock of Your present Financial Situation:

Examine your present financial situation. Calculate your earnings, spending, and assets and liabilities. This evaluation will provide you with a full picture of your financial health and will assist you in identifying areas that need improvement.

Creating a Realistic Budget:

Create a budget that is in line with your income and financial objectives. Divide your spending into two categories: fixed (e.g., rent, utilities) and variable (e.g., entertainment, eating out). Set aside a percentage of your earnings for savings and investing. Make sure your budget provides for flexibility and allows for unforeseen costs.

Tracking Your Spending:

Keep a close eye on your spending patterns. Maintain a record of your spending, either manually or via the use of budgeting applications and tools. This technique enables you to discover areas where you may be overpaying and make the required changes to remain within your budget.

Making Saving and an Emergency Fund a

Priority:

Make saving a priority. Set aside a percentage of your salary for savings, with the goal of accumulating an emergency fund that can cover three to six months of living costs. This fund serves as a safety net in the event of unanticipated events, offering financial stability and peace of mind.

Debt Management:

If you have previous debts, create a plan to manage and pay them off. Prioritize high-interest obligations and look into debt consolidation or refinancing to lower interest rates. Reduce your usage of credit cards and concentrate on good credit management.

Creating an Investment Strategy:

Plan for your future by intelligently investing your money. Consider your risk tolerance and investing objectives while researching alternative investment choices such as stocks, bonds, mutual funds, or real estate. Consult a financial adviser if necessary to build an investing strategy that meets your requirements.

Reviewing and Adjusting Your Plan:

Review your financial plan and budget on a regular basis to verify they are in line with your current circumstances and objectives. Because life circumstances vary, so should your financial strategy. Make modifications as required and be proactive in your financial management.

Seeking Professional Advice:

If you are overwhelmed by financial planning and budgeting, or if you have a complicated financial position, seek the advice of a professional financial planner. They may provide you specialized counsel, assist you in optimizing your financial strategy, and offer assistance on tax planning and asset management.

Creating Healthy Financial Habits:

Develop healthy financial habits that complement your objectives. Practicing disciplined spending, avoiding excessive debt, automating bill payments and savings contributions, and remaining knowledgeable about personal financial subjects are all part of this.

Budgeting and financial planning are constant procedures. You can take charge of your financial destiny and strive toward your desired results by actively managing your funds and making educated choices. Maintain your commitment to your goal, be adaptive to changes, and evaluate your progress on a frequent basis. You can lay a solid financial foundation and pave the road for long-term financial success with time, dedication, and a proactive approach.

Investing For Long-Term Success:

Investing is an important part of creating long-term wealth and financial success. It entails deliberately allocating your money to assets with the potential to appreciate in value over time. Whether you're a novice or a seasoned investor, here are some key ideas to consider when investing for long-term success:

Set Specific Financial Goals:

Before you begin investing, identify your financial objectives. Are you putting money down for your retirement, a down payment on a home, or your child's education? Understanding your objectives can assist you in determining the proper investment period and risk tolerance.

Educate Yourself:

Spend time learning about various investing opportunities, their risks, and possible rewards. Read books, go to seminars, and keep up with trustworthy financial news sources. The more you learn, the more prepared you will be to make sound investing choices.

Diversify Your Portfolio:

Diversification is essential for risk management and optimizing profits. Invest in a variety of asset types, such as stocks, bonds, real estate, and mutual funds. Consider diversifying further within each asset class by investing in different sectors or areas.

Invest Over Time:

Investing is a marathon, not a sprint. Long-term investment enables you to benefit from compounding gains while weathering short-term market swings. Avoid making frequent adjustments to your portfolio based on short-term market swings.

Determine Your Risk Tolerance:

Before investing, evaluate your risk tolerance. Determine your tolerance for volatility and your level of comfort with probable variations in your investment results. Your asset allocation selections will be guided by your risk tolerance.

Consider Tax-Saving Strategies:

Take into account the tax consequences of your investments. To optimize your tax advantages, choose tax-advantaged funds such as individual retirement accounts (IRAs) and 401(k)s. Consult a tax specialist to learn how to organize your investments to be tax-efficient.

Invest in Index Funds or ETFs:

If you're new to investing or prefer a hands-off approach, index funds or exchange-traded funds (ETFs) are good options. These products are designed to mirror a certain market index while providing wide market exposure at a reasonable cost.

Dollar-Cost Averaging:

Use a dollar-cost averaging approach to invest a certain amount of money at regular periods. This strategy reduces market volatility by purchasing more shares when prices are low and fewer shares when prices are high.

Rebalance Your Portfolio:

Review and rebalance your investment portfolio on a regular basis to ensure it is aligned with your asset allocation goals. Certain assets may outperform or underperform over time, leading your portfolio to diverge from the asset composition you prefer.

Seek Professional Advice:

Consult a professional financial planner or investment adviser for individualized advice based on your financial objectives, risk tolerance, and investment timeline. They can assist you in developing a thorough investment strategy and give continuous guidance.

Remember that investing entails risks and that there are no guarantees of profits. Maintain your knowledge, be patient, and avoid making rash judgments based on short-term market changes. Investing for long-term wealth involves discipline, diversity, and dedication to your financial objectives. You may establish a firm basis for long-term financial development and wealth by following these tactics and customizing them to your own circumstances.

Creating Multiple Income Streams: Creating Multiple Income Streams

Having numerous sources of income may bring financial stability, security, and even prospects for wealth building in today's volatile and unpredictable economic world. Creating several streams of income entails diversifying your revenue sources to lessen your dependency on a single wage or company enterprise. Here are some ways to explore if you want to create various revenue streams:

Identify Your Unique Skills, Talents, and Areas of knowledge:

Begin by recognizing your unique skills, talents, and areas of knowledge. What do you find interesting? What are your strong points? Consider your abilities and how you may use them to generate other revenue sources.

Investigate Freelancing and Consulting:

Offer your skills as a freelancer or consultant in your field. Many firms and individuals are ready to pay on a project basis for specific talents. Platforms such as Upwork, Freelancer, and Fiverr allow you to connect with customers looking for specialized skills.

Start an Online company:

There are several options to start and expand an online company. Consider starting an e-commerce business, selling digital goods or services, or monetizing your blog or YouTube channel. The internet world offers a worldwide marketplace as well as the opportunity for scalable revenue.

Invest in Real Estate:

Real estate may be a great way to generate passive income. Investigate options to invest in residential or commercial rental properties. Rental income may offer a consistent source of income, and property appreciation can grow your wealth over time.

Create and Monetize material:

Consider monetizing your material if you have a flair for writing, making videos, or producing podcasts. Ad revenue, subscriptions, memberships, and sponsorships are all ways to generate money on platforms like YouTube, Patreon, and podcast sponsorships.

Invest in equities and Dividend-Paying Assets:

To produce passive income via capital appreciation and dividend payments, invest in equities, exchange-traded funds (ETFs), or dividend-paying assets. To make educated investing selections that match with your risk tolerance and financial objectives, do research and talk with a financial adviser.

Rental Income & Property Sharing:

Consider renting out excess space in your house or property on services such as Airbnb or VRBO. By leveraging your current assets, you may generate more money.

Make and Sell Online Courses or Information goods:

If you have experience in a certain sector, think about making and selling online courses or information goods. Platforms such as Udemy and Teachable enable you to reach a large audience and earn money from your knowledge and experience.

Create Royalty Income Streams:

If you have artistic abilities such as writing, music, or painting, look into earning royalties. Create a book, license your music, or sell digital art on the internet. As your works continue to sell, royalties might bring recurring money.

Join respectable network marketing or affiliate marketing programs that correspond with your interests and principles. You may make money by marketing and selling items or services to your network or audience via these programs.

Remember that creating various sources of income takes time, effort, and a willingness to try new things. Establishing and growing each revenue source may take time, so be patient and persistent. Diversify your sources of income to reduce risk and build a more robust financial base. You may establish numerous sources of income that contribute to your financial well-being and open doors to greater financial independence with careful preparation, smart execution, and a proactive mentality.

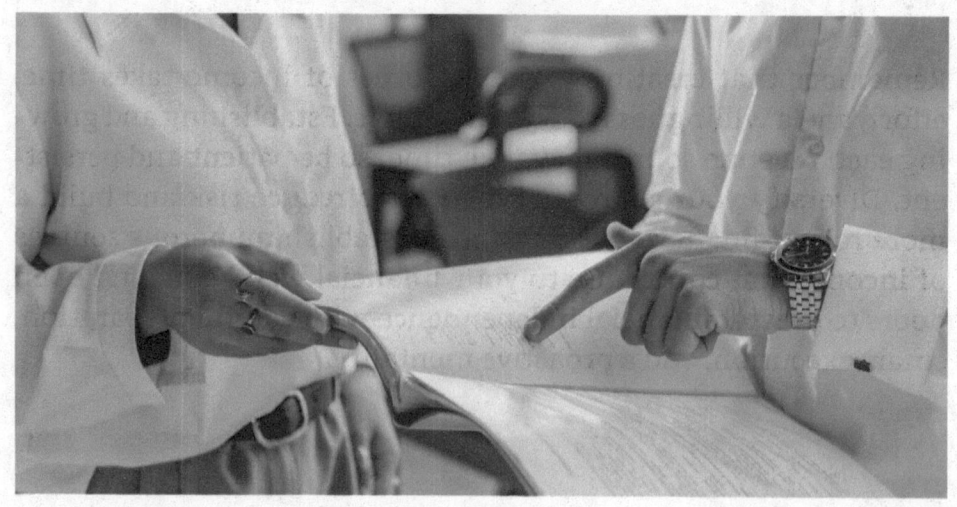

CHAPTER 7: OVERCOMING FINANCIAL CHALLENGES

Managing Debt And Financial Hurdles.

F inancial hurdles and debt may have a negative impact on your financial health and prevent you from achieving financial independence. However, you can manage debt and get through financial challenges if you have the correct tactics and attitude. Here are some crucial actions to think about:

Assess Your Debt:

Begin by doing a debt assessment. Make a note of all your unpaid credit card bills, outstanding loans, and other debts. Include each debt's interest rates, required minimum payments, and total amount still owed. You'll have a comprehensive understanding of your debt condition after this assessment.

Establish a Budget:

Setting up a budget is essential for successfully managing your money. Keep track of your earnings and outgoing costs, and set aside some of your money for debt repayment. Find places where you might reduce spending to generate extra funds for debt reduction.

Set a priority for your debt repayment once you've established a budget:

The debt avalanche technique and the debt snowball method are the two often used strategies. The debt snowball approach starts by paying off the smallest bills first whereas the debt avalanche method prioritizes paying off the debts with the highest interest rates first. Pick a strategy that supports your monetary objectives and inspires you.

Negotiate with Creditors:

If you're having trouble paying your bills or are having financial difficulties, you may want to talk to your creditors. They could be open to negotiating a lower interest rate, waiving fees, or coming up with a more reasonable payback schedule in certain circumstances. Ask for their help and be honest about your circumstance.

Consolidate or Refinance Debt:

Refinancing an existing loan or combining many loans into one might streamline your repayment procedure and perhaps result in cheaper interest rates. To consolidate or refinance your debt, consider choices like personal loans, balance transfer credit cards, or home equity loans.

Seek Professional Advice:

If you're drowning in debt or dealing with complicated financial issues, think about getting assistance from a credit counseling organization or a financial counselor. They may provide you individualized advice, assist you in developing a debt management strategy, and deal with creditors on your behalf.

Create an Emergency Fund:

In the case of unforeseen bills or crises, having an emergency fund serves as a financial safety net and prevents you from taking on further debt. Build up your emergency fund over time by starting with a modest amount of your salary each month and saving enough to last for at least three to six months of living costs.

Take a deeper look at your spending patterns and financial behavior to improve your financial habits. Determine any tendencies or actions that may have exacerbated your debt or other financial difficulties. Create better financial habits by limiting wasteful spending, exercising restraint with your money, and saving for future costs rather than using credit.

Focus on Financial Education:

Make time to improve your financial literacy. Take online classes, attend seminars, or read books on generating wealth, managing debt, and setting up a budget. You'll be better able to make wise financial choices the more educated you are.

Maintain a Positive Attitude and Stay Motivated:

Overcoming debt and financial hurdles might be difficult, but doing so requires persistence and keeping motivated. Celebrate minor accomplishments along the road, enlist the help of loved ones, and picture the financial independence you want. Keep in mind that development takes time, and that each action moves you one step closer to your objectives.

Debt management and conquering financial challenges take dedication, self-control, and tenacity. You may recover control of your money and pave the road for a more secure and profitable financial future by putting these tactics into practice and being committed to your financial objectives.

Developing Resilience in the Face of Setbacks:

Life is full of unforeseen obstacles, and overcoming them is a crucial component of being financially successful. Resilience development is essential for overcoming obstacles and keeping a positive outlook. Resilience is the capacity to recover and adapt in the face of adversity. Here are some techniques that aid in developing resilience:

Reframe Setbacks as Learning Opportunities:

Reframe setbacks as worthwhile learning opportunities rather than seeing them as failures. Recognize that failures are a normal part of the road to financial success and that they teach you important lessons for development. Adopt a development attitude that views obstacles as opportunities to advance.

Develop an optimistic Attitude:

Resilience can only be developed by being optimistic. Pay attention to the parts of your financial journey that are going well, and express thanks for your accomplishments. Teach yourself to see barriers as transient challenges rather than insurmountable ones. Find supportive people and inspiring accounts of those who have overcame hardship to surround oneself with.

Develop emotional awareness by being aware of your feelings when you encounter obstacles:

Feelings of annoyance, dissatisfaction, or worry are common. Allow yourself to feel these feelings, but also work on your self-care and self-compassion. Spend time in nature, practice meditation, or engage in other stress-relieving activities.

Develop a Supportive Network:

Surround yourself with a network of family, friends, mentors, or others who share your values in order to get support when things go tough. Ask for guidance from them and be honest about your experiences. You may overcome obstacles more successfully as a team and lean on one another for support.

Practice Adaptability:

When faced with obstacles, flexibility and adaptability are crucial traits. Be willing to change your expectations, techniques, or plans as necessary. Accept change and view it as a chance to advance.

You may uncover new avenues for success and lessen the effects of failures by adjusting to new situations.

Focus on Finding answers, Not Problems:

Refocus your attention on finding answers rather than obsessing on the obstacles themselves. Take proactive measures to overcome the obstacles by doing an objective analysis of the problem and coming up with feasible solutions. Larger issues should be broken down into smaller, more manageable tasks, and minor victories should be celebrated along the way.

Keep a Long-Term Perspective:

On a longer trip, failures are often just momentary setbacks. Remind yourself of the wider picture and your long-term objectives. Recognize that failures are a necessary part of the process and may provide chances for learning and development. Remain dedicated to your financial goals and have a positive outlook, understanding that failures do not determine your eventual success.

Embrace the idea of "failing forward" by utilizing your mistakes as stepping stones to success by learning from them and adapting. Consider your mistakes, pinpoint your development opportunities, and make the appropriate corrections. Refine your tactics, learn new talents, and broaden your financial knowledge by taking advantage of losses.

Self-care is important for resilience development.

You should take care of your physical, mental, and emotional well-being. Give self-care activities a high priority so you may recharge and be renewed. Make time for your interests, rest, and close relationships. Taking care of your general well-being will give you the strength and fortitude to confront obstacles head-on.

Celebrate Even the Smallest Victories:

As you progress financially, rejoice in all of your accomplishments. Recognize and appreciate your progress, regardless of how little it may appear. You may maintain a happy outlook, increase your drive, and become more resilient by celebrating minor triumphs.

Keep in mind that failures do not determine your financial destiny; they are just temporary. You may overcome obstacles with grace and come out stronger and more motivated to reach your financial objectives by developing resilience, maintaining a positive outlook, and using setbacks as teaching opportunities.

Changing Your Money Thinking During Difficult Circumstances.

Difficult circumstances often put our money thinking to the test and put our thoughts and attitudes about money to the test. These challenging times, nevertheless, also provide a chance for personal development and change. You may create a better connection with money and put yourself in a position for long-term financial success by actively striving to change your money perspective during challenging circumstances. You may use the following tactics to aid you in this process:

Recognize Your present Money mentality:

Begin by recognizing your present money mentality, including the ideas and values you have about money. Do you tend to think in terms of scarcity or do you think in terms of abundance? Are possibilities motivating you more than fear? Knowing your present financial perspective is crucial for figuring out what needs to change.

Examine and Disprove restricting ideas:

Consider and disprove any restricting ideas you may have around money. Some examples of these ideas include "Money is scarce," "I'm not good with money," or "I'll never be wealthy." Use uplifting affirmations and words that assist your financial development and wealth to dispel these limiting thoughts. Transform your negative self-talk into empowered and uplifting ideas.

Develop an attitude of thankfulness and plenty by practicing it, especially during difficult circumstances. Consider your assets rather than your shortcomings. Recognize your financial situation's advantages on a regular basis, no matter how little they may be. You may attract more advantageous situations and make yourself more financially abundant by changing your emphasis to abundance.

Embrace Financial Education:

Take advantage of adversity to increase your financial awareness and understanding. Learn about budgeting, investing, personal finance, and money management. The more you know about money, the more confident you'll feel in your ability to make wise financial choices. Look for publications, audiobooks, online courses, and seminars that provide beneficial financial education.

Develop Realistic and Empowering Financial objectives:

It's important to develop realistic and empowering financial objectives during challenging circumstances. Divide your objectives into smaller, more doable milestones that you can reach given your existing situation. Celebrate each accomplishment because doing so helps you have a good attitude towards money and keeps you inspired to keep going.

Spending with awareness:

Pay attention to your spending patterns and make sure they support your financial objectives. Make thoughtful choices regarding your spending and stay away from impulsive purchases. Put your necessities above your desires and, where necessary, learn to wait gratification. Spending with awareness enables you to match your behavior to your financial goals.

Embrace optimistic Influences:

Surround yourself with people that have a healthy and optimistic attitude about money. Talk about money with like-minded individuals who encourage and inspire you. Find coaches, mentors, or financial advisers who can provide help and direction through challenging times. Your financial perspective may change as a result of their beneficial effect.

Self-care and stress management are essential during trying times, so practice these two skills.

Make self-care activities a priority that may help you feel better emotionally and minimize stress. Exercise, journal writing, meditation, and spending time with loved ones are a few things to try. When you put self-care first, you improve your resilience and provide the groundwork for changing your financial perspective.

Visualize Financial Success:

Use visualization techniques to see yourself as financially successful. Make a clear mental image of your intended financial results and experience the satisfying feelings that come with reaching those objectives. By reprogramming your subconscious mind and reinforcing a good money perspective, visualization makes it simpler to realize your financial goals.

Practice Being Generous and Giving:

Perform acts of kindness and generosity, no matter how tiny. Sharing your abilities, time, or resources with others helps you to feel abundant and broadens your perspective on money. Contribute to causes or groups that share your beliefs. By being generous, you strengthen the idea that there is always enough to go around and that money may be used to make a good difference.

It takes time, perseverance, and introspection to change your money perspective when things are tough. Use the difficulties to redefine your connection with money by accepting them as chances for personal development. You may develop a better, more empowered money attitude that promotes your long-term financial well-being with patience and deliberate work.

CHAPTER 8: NURTURING YOUR MONEY MAGNET LIFESTYLE

Managing Debt And Financial Hurdles.

Financial hurdles and debt may have a negative impact on your financial health and prevent you from achieving financial independence. However, you can manage debt and get through financial challenges if you have the correct tactics and attitude. Here are some crucial actions to think about:

Assess Your Debt:

Begin by doing a debt assessment. Make a note of all your unpaid credit card bills, outstanding loans, and other debts. Include each debt's interest rates, required minimum payments, and total amount still owed. You'll have a comprehensive understanding of your debt condition after this assessment.

Establish a Budget:

Setting up a budget is essential for successfully managing your money. Keep track of your earnings and outgoing costs, and set aside some of your money for debt repayment. Find places where you might reduce spending to generate extra funds for debt reduction.

Set a priority for your debt repayment once you've established a budget.

The debt avalanche technique and the debt snowball method are the two often used strategies. The debt snowball approach starts by paying off the smallest bills first whereas the debt avalanche method prioritizes paying off the debts with the highest interest rates first. Pick a strategy that supports your monetary objectives and inspires you.

Negotiate with Creditors:

If you're having trouble paying your bills or are having financial difficulties, you may want to talk to your creditors. They could be open to negotiating a lower interest rate, waiving fees, or coming up with a more reasonable payback schedule in certain circumstances. Ask for their help and be honest about your circumstance.

Consolidate or Refinance Debt: Refinancing an existing loan or combining many loans into one might streamline your repayment procedure and perhaps result in cheaper interest rates. To consolidate or refinance your debt, consider choices like personal loans, balance transfer credit cards, or home equity loans.

Seek Professional Advice:

If you're drowning in debt or dealing with complicated financial issues, think about getting assistance from a credit counseling organization or a financial counselor. They may provide you individualized advice, assist you in developing a debt management strategy, and deal with creditors on your behalf.

Create an Emergency Fund:

In the case of unforeseen bills or crises, having an emergency fund serves as a financial safety net and prevents you from taking on further debt. Build up your emergency fund over time by starting with a modest amount of your salary each month and saving enough to last for at least three to six months of living costs.

Take a deeper look at your spending patterns and financial behavior to improve your financial habits.

Determine any tendencies or actions that may have exacerbated your debt or other financial difficulties. Create better financial habits by limiting wasteful spending, exercising restraint with your money, and saving for future costs rather than using credit.

Focus on Financial Education:

Make time to improve your financial literacy. Take online classes, attend seminars, or read books on generating wealth, managing debt, and setting up a budget. You'll be better able to make wise financial choices the more educated you are.

Maintain a Positive Attitude and Stay Motivated:

Overcoming debt and financial hurdles might be difficult, but doing so requires persistence and keeping motivated. Celebrate minor accomplishments along the road, enlist the help of loved ones, and picture the financial independence you want. Keep in mind that development takes time, and that each action moves you one step closer to your objectives.

Debt management and conquering financial challenges take dedication, self-control, and tenacity. You may recover control of your money and pave the road for a more secure and profitable financial future by putting these tactics into practice and being committed to your financial objectives.

Developing Resilience In The Face Of Setbacks.

Life is full of unforeseen obstacles, and overcoming them is a crucial component of being financially successful. Resilience development is essential for overcoming obstacles and keeping a positive outlook. Resilience is the capacity to recover and adapt in the face of adversity. Here are some techniques that aid in developing resilience:

Reframe Setbacks as Learning Opportunities:

Reframe setbacks as worthwhile learning opportunities rather than seeing them as failures. Recognize that failures are a normal part of the road to financial success and that they teach you important lessons for development. Adopt a development attitude that views obstacles as opportunities to advance.

Develop an optimistic Attitude:

Resilience can only be developed by being optimistic. Pay attention to the parts of your financial journey that are going well, and express thanks for your accomplishments. Teach yourself to see barriers as transient challenges rather than insurmountable ones. Find supportive people and inspiring accounts of those who have overcame hardship to surround oneself with.

Develop emotional awareness by being aware of your feelings when you encounter obstacles. Feelings of annoyance, dissatisfaction, or worry are common. Allow yourself to feel these feelings, but also work on your self-care and self-compassion. Spend time in nature, practice meditation, or engage in other stress-relieving activities.

Develop a Supportive Network:

Surround yourself with a network of family, friends, mentors, or others who share your values in order to get support when things go tough. Ask for guidance from them and be honest about your experiences. You may overcome obstacles more successfully as a team and lean on one another for support.

Practice Adaptability:

When faced with obstacles, flexibility and adaptability are crucial traits. Be willing to change your expectations, techniques, or plans as necessary. Accept change and view it as a chance to advance. You may uncover new avenues for success and lessen the effects of failures by adjusting to new situations.

Focus on Finding answers, Not Problems:

Refocus your attention on finding answers rather than obsessing on the obstacles themselves. Take proactive measures to overcome the obstacles by doing an objective analysis of the problem and coming up with feasible solutions. Larger issues should be broken down into smaller, more manageable tasks, and minor victories should be celebrated along the way.

Keep a Long-Term Perspective:

On a longer trip, failures are often just momentary setbacks. Remind yourself of the wider picture and your long-term objectives. Recognize that failures are a necessary part of the process and may provide chances for learning and development. Remain dedicated to your financial goals and have a positive outlook, understanding that failures do not determine your eventual success.

Embrace the idea of "failing forward" by utilizing your mistakes as stepping stones to success by learning from them and adapting. Consider your mistakes, pinpoint your development opportunities, and make the appropriate corrections. Refine your tactics, learn new talents, and broaden your financial knowledge by taking advantage of losses.

Self-care is important for resilience development.

You should take care of your physical, mental, and emotional well-being. Give self-care activities a high priority so you may recharge and be renewed. Make time for your interests, rest, and close relationships. Taking care of your general well-being will give you the strength and fortitude to confront obstacles head-on.

Celebrate Even the Smallest Victories:

As you progress financially, rejoice in all of your accomplishments. Recognize and appreciate your progress, regardless of how little it may appear. You may maintain a happy outlook, increase your drive, and become more resilient by celebrating minor triumphs.

Keep in mind that failures do not determine your financial destiny; they are just temporary. You may overcome obstacles with grace and come out stronger and more motivated to reach your financial objectives by developing resilience, maintaining a positive outlook, and using setbacks as teaching opportunities.

Changing Your Money Thinking During Difficult Circumstances.

Difficult circumstances often put our money thinking to the test and put our thoughts and attitudes about money to the test. These challenging times, nevertheless, also provide a chance for personal development and change. You may create a better connection with money and put yourself in a position for long-term financial success by actively striving to change your money perspective during challenging circumstances. You may use the following tactics to aid you in this process:

Recognize Your present Money mentality:

Begin by recognizing your present money mentality, including the ideas and values you have about money. Do you tend to think in terms of scarcity or do you think in terms of abundance? Are possibilities motivating you more than fear? Knowing your present financial perspective is crucial for figuring out what needs to change.

Examine and Disprove restricting ideas:

Consider and disprove any restricting ideas you may have around money. Some examples of these ideas include "Money is scarce," "I'm not good with money," or "I'll never be wealthy." Use uplifting affirmations and words that assist your financial development and wealth to dispel these limiting thoughts. Transform your negative self-talk into empowered and uplifting ideas.

Develop an attitude of thankfulness and plenty by practicing it, especially during difficult circumstances. Consider your assets rather than your shortcomings. Recognize your financial situation's advantages on a regular basis, no matter how little they may be. You may attract more advantageous situations and make yourself more financially abundant by changing your emphasis to abundance.

Embrace Financial Education:

Take advantage of adversity to increase your financial awareness and understanding. Learn about budgeting, investing, personal finance, and money management. The more you know about money, the more confident you'll feel in your ability to make wise financial choices. Look for publications, audiobooks, online courses, and seminars that provide beneficial financial education.

Develop Realistic and Empowering Financial objectives:

It's important to develop realistic and empowering financial objectives during challenging circumstances. Divide your objectives into smaller, more doable milestones that you can reach given your existing situation. Celebrate each accomplishment because doing so helps you have a good attitude towards money and keeps you inspired to keep going.

Spending with awareness: Pay attention to your spending patterns and make sure they support your financial objectives. Make thoughtful choices regarding your spending and stay away from impulsive purchases. Put your necessities above your desires and, where necessary, learn to wait gratification. Spending with awareness enables you to match your behavior to your financial goals.

Embrace optimistic Influences:

Surround yourself with people that have a healthy and optimistic attitude about money. Talk about money with like-minded individuals who encourage and inspire you. Find coaches, mentors, or financial advisers who can provide help and direction through challenging times. Your financial perspective may change as a result of their beneficial effect.

Self-care and stress management are essential during trying times, so practice these two skills. Make self-care activities a priority that may help you feel better emotionally and minimize stress. Exercise, journal writing, meditation, and spending time with loved ones are a few things to try. When you put self-care first, you improve your resilience and provide the groundwork for changing your financial perspective.

Visualize Financial Success:

Use visualization techniques to see yourself as financially successful. Make a clear mental image of your intended financial results and experience the satisfying feelings that come with reaching those objectives. By reprogramming your subconscious mind and reinforcing a good money perspective, visualization makes it simpler to realize your financial goals.

Practice Being Generous and Giving:

Perform acts of kindness and generosity, no matter how tiny. Sharing your abilities, time, or resources with others helps you to feel abundant and broadens your perspective on money. Contribute to causes or groups that share your beliefs. By being generous, you strengthen the idea that there is always enough to go around and that money may be used to make a good difference.

It takes time, perseverance, and introspection to change your money perspective when things are tough. Use the difficulties to redefine your connection with money by accepting them as chances for personal development. You may develop a better, more empowered money attitude that promotes your long-term financial well-being with patience and deliberate work.

CHAPTER 9: CONCLUSION

Embracing Your Money Magnet Potential.

Have you ever wondered why some individuals appear to easily attract money and prosperity while others struggle to make ends meet? It's not a matter of chance or coincidence; it's all about embracing your money magnet potential. Yes, you have the ability to attract and actualize financial abundance. So, let's look at how you might tap into this enormous potential and build a money magnet field around you.

It all begins with your thinking, first and foremost. You must think that money is a good factor in your life and that you are worthy of it. Allow yourself to let go of any negative ideas or scarcity thinking that is holding you back. Adopt an abundant attitude instead, in which you see chances and potential everywhere. Remember that your ideas and beliefs affect your reality, so adopt beliefs that empower you and correspond with your financial objectives.

Following that, it is critical to link your behaviors with your financial goals. Set specific objectives and devise a plan of action to attain them. Divide your objectives into smaller, more attainable stages and take regular action toward them. Be proactive in pursuing possibilities that correspond with your financial objectives, whether it's beginning a side company, investing in your education, or looking out additional income sources. Taking action communicates to the universe that you are serious about attracting prosperity.

When it comes to embracing your money magnet potential, visualization is a powerful tool. Spend some time each day visualizing yourself enjoying the life of financial wealth you want. Imagine yourself surrounded by money, enjoying the freedom and pleasure that it gives. Feel thankfulness, enthusiasm, and satisfaction as though it were actually occurring. Visualization trains your subconscious mind to attract chances and situations that are in line with your financial objectives. It's like sowing plenty seeds in your imagination, which will develop and materialize in your reality.

Affirmations, in addition to imagery, may boost your money magnet potential. Affirmations are positive phrases that you tell yourself on a daily basis. They assist in rewiring your subconscious mind with positive money and wealth attitudes. Affirmations such as "I am a magnet for money and abundance," "I effortlessly attract wealth," and "I deserve to be financially prosperous" are examples. Repeat these affirmations with conviction and confidence, and see how they influence your thoughts and behavior.

Being open to receiving is another important component of embracing your money magnet potential. We might unwittingly obstruct the flow of plenty by holding restrictive thoughts about receiving. Practice making oneself available to receive money and possibilities. Let rid of any feelings of shame or unworthiness that come with obtaining money. Recognize that wealth is intended for you, and that by receiving, you can also give back and have a great effect on the world. The more open you are to receiving, the more the universe can provide to you.

Finally, surround yourself with good influences and people who share your values. Seek for mentors, coaches, or friends who have embraced their money magnet potential and are enjoying a prosperous life. Learn from their mistakes, absorb their wisdom, and use their good energy to elevate and motivate you. Surrounding yourself with a supportive group may help to reaffirm your views, fuel your drive, and give useful insights as you continue on your path to financial success.

Embracing your money magnet potential does not imply pursuing money for the purpose of chasing money. It is all about living a life of freedom, affluence, and satisfaction. It's about utilizing your money to live your mission, assist your loved ones, and make a difference in the world. Take a time to consider your personal money magnet potential. Have faith in your own potential to attract and materialize money. Take consistent action, imagine your desired results, repeat powerful affirmations, and remain open to receiving. With these techniques, you may tap into your full money magnet potential and live a life of plenty beyond your wildest dreams.

Sustaining Financial Success with Mantras:

Financial success is more than just meeting particular objectives or reaching certain milestones; it is also about maintaining that success over time. While there are many different techniques and tactics for managing and improving one's money, including mantras into one's financial path may be a great tool for preserving and boosting financial success. Positive affirmations or phrases known as mantras may assist transform mindsets and align ideas with desired objectives. In this article, we will look at the function of mantras in financial success and how they may be used in everyday life.

The Mindset Effect:

One of the primary advantages of employing mantras in finance is their capacity to build a positive and empowered mentality. Financial success is driven not just by statistics, but also by money-related ideas, attitudes, and emotions. Mantras may aid in the removal of limiting ideas and negative mental patterns that impede advancement. By actively repeating positive financial mantras such as "I am worthy of financial abundance" or "I attract wealth and prosperity," people may rewire their subconscious thoughts and build attitudes favorable to long-term financial success.

Practice and consistency:

When implementing mantras into a financial path, consistency is essential. Repeating selected mantras on a regular basis, particularly in the morning or before participating in financial activities, sets the tone for the day and aligns thoughts and actions with financial objectives. Individuals utilize their positive energy to infiltrate their mind and impact their financial choices and actions by repeating mantras with conviction and confidence. Mantra practice that is consistent maintains the right mentality and develops the basis for long-term financial success.

Motivation and concentration:

Mantras may also assist people in staying focused and motivated on their financial goals. Financial success requires discipline and endurance, particularly during difficult circumstances. Individuals who use mantras that reinforce resolve and resilience, such as "I am committed to my financial goals" or "I overcome obstacles and thrive financially," develop a solid internal foundation that supports future success. When confronted with setbacks or diversions, mantras serve as regular reminders of financial goals and sources of inspiration and motivation.

Authenticity and personalization:

It is critical to choose mantras that are unique to you and represent your financial objectives and ideals. Every person's financial path is different, and what works for one person may not work for another. Reflecting on personal financial objectives, principles, and areas that need support or encouragement enables the creation of true and meaningful mantras. Mantras become strong instruments for maintaining financial success when they fit with personal ambitions because they hold significant importance and resonate on a deeper level.

Mantras as Catalysts, Not Replacements:

It is critical to remember that slogans are not a replacement for action. While they may accelerate good transformation and mental improvements, taking real measures to attain financial objectives is required. Mantras give motivation and direction while making financial choices, maintaining budgets, investing, and seeking new chances for development. Combining the power of mantras with educated action results in a comprehensive strategy to long-term financial success.

Conclusion:

Mantras may help you maintain financial success by fostering a good mentality, offering inspiration, and connecting your thoughts and actions with your financial objectives. Individuals that incorporate mantras into their everyday lives and continuously repeat them reinforce powerful thoughts, overcome limiting beliefs, and remain focused on their financial goal.

Mantras that are personalized and real that resonate deeply are very effective. It is important to remember, however, that mantras are not stand-alone answers; they should be employed in conjunction with real steps and activities. Individuals may continue their financial success and establish a meaningful and profitable financial future by combining a positive mentality with educated action.

Including Others In Your Wealth Journey.

A wealth journey is a chance to empower and inspire others along the route, not only for personal benefit. You have the opportunity to have a beneficial influence on the lives of others as you collect riches and achieve financial success, promoting a feeling of empowerment and providing chances for advancement. In this article, we will look at the importance of empowering others as you go through your wealth path, as well as many ways you may make a difference in the lives of others around you.

Education and Mentorship:

Sharing your expertise and experiences is a great approach to empower others. Consider being a mentor or providing educational chances to those who might benefit from your knowledge. You may help people manage their own financial journeys and make educated choices by giving direction, support, and important insights. Empowering people via education and mentoring has a positive ripple effect as they pass on their knowledge to others, resulting in a circle of progress and empowerment.

Philanthropy and charity Giving:

Philanthropy and charity giving allow people to support causes and organizations that have a beneficial influence on society. You may donate to efforts that connect with your beliefs and solve major social, environmental, or humanitarian challenges by donating a percentage of your money to charitable activities. Your financial resources may make genuine change and empower people in need, whether you donate to charity organizations, establish foundations, or actively participate in fundraising activities.

Social entrepreneurship entails using your money and entrepreneurial talents to build long-term, socially responsible enterprises. Social entrepreneurship is the use of company initiatives to solve social or environmental issues while making a profit. You may empower individuals and communities by offering job opportunities, supporting local economies, and adopting sustainable practices by concentrating on business models that value people and the world. Social entrepreneurship blends financial success with good social impact, resulting in an effective platform for empowerment.

Financial Education and Literacy:

Financial literacy is a crucial skill that enables people to make educated financial choices and take charge of their financial well-being. Consider investing in financial literacy programs or projects, especially in marginalized populations. Individuals are empowered to break the cycle of financial insecurity and build a brighter future for themselves and their family when they are given the information and skills to handle their resources efficiently.

Collaboration and Networks:

Collaboration is an important part of empowerment. Seek collaboration possibilities with like-minded people, organizations, or networks that share your goal of empowerment via wealth. By combining your resources, experience, and networks, you can collectively have a larger effect and expand the reach of your activities. Collaboration allows for the sharing of ideas, support, and group problem-solving, resulting in a more powerful and effective force for empowerment.

Being an inspirational example is one of the most effective methods to encourage people. In your financial path, demonstrate integrity, compassion, and ethical decision-making. Share your narrative, both your accomplishments and your setbacks, in order to inspire and encourage others. You may light the flame of empowerment in others and motivate them to achieve their own goals and aspirations by displaying the possibilities and potential that come with financial success.

Finally, inspiring people via your wealth path extends beyond your own financial achievement. You may make a significant difference in the lives of others by sharing your expertise, participating in charity, embracing social entrepreneurship, encouraging financial education, developing collaborative relationships, and leading by example. Empowerment is more than just having money; it is about using your riches, talents, and influence to elevate and create possibilities for progress in the lives of others around you. Accept the responsibility and privilege that money brings, and utilize it to effect good change and empowerment in our world.

EPILOGUE

As we reach the end of this changing journey through "The Money Magnet Mantras: A Step-by-Step Guide to Making and Retaining Money," it's time to reflect on the amazing progress we've made and the deep changes that have occurred in our lives.

Throughout this book, we studied the intricate link between our attitude, our actions, and our financial abundance. We dove into the core principles and practical techniques that enable us to attract and keep wealth. By embracing the power of our ideas and aligning them with our goals, we found the real potential within ourselves to become money magnets.

As we applied the money magnet mantras and incorporated them into our daily lives, we watched amazing transformations taking place. We went from a scarcity mindset to an abundance mindset, accepting the belief that wealth and success are available to us in limitless amounts. By cultivating thanks for what we already possess and visualizing our financial goals with unwavering clarity, we sparked a powerful force that attracted wealth towards us.

Moreover, we learned the importance of taking thoughtful and constant action towards our financial goals. By adopting strict habits such as planning, saving, and investing, we set a strong basis for long-term financial success. We knew that each financial choice we made was a chance to move closer to our aspirations.

In addition, we discussed the significance of cultivating a good relationship with money. We understood that money is a tool that can be used to build a life of purpose, joy, and fulfillment. By knowing our values, defining our financial goals, and aligning our financial choices with our authentic selves, we made a harmonious relationship with money that improved our general well-being.

As we flip through the pages of our financial trip, we may find that we faced hurdles and setbacks along the way. However, armed with the information and wisdom gained from this book, we learned to view these hurdles as stepping stones towards growth. We accepted the power of resiliency, perseverance, and adaptability, and in doing so, we overcame obstacles that once seemed impossible.

Now, as we come to the end of this book, it is important to remember that the trip doesn't stop here. The money magnet chants are not a one-time practice but a lifelong pledge to our financial well-being. We must continue to nurture our thoughts, actions, and beliefs to line with our goals, always staying open to the chances that present themselves.

Remember, each day offers a chance to make conscious choices that drive us towards financial wealth. So, as you close this book, take a moment to think on the progress you've made and the transformations that have happened. Celebrate your successes and commit to further growth and development in all areas of your life.

May the money magnet mantras continue to guide you on your path to financial success and may you live a life filled with prosperity, joy, and the freedom that comes from being a true money magnet.

With heartfelt gratitude,

Mohd Faisal

ABOUT THE AUTHOR

Mohd Faisal

Mohd Faisal, an accomplished Indian author, has captivated readers worldwide with his profound works on personal growth, relationships, and spirituality. His unique perspective connects readers from all backgrounds, thanks to his deep understanding of human psychology and caring attitude. Faisal has established himself as a trusted voice in the self-help field, simplifying complex concepts into practical recommendations. His publications explore the complexities of the human mind and offer strategies for navigating life's obstacles. Faisal's work reflects a genuine desire to help others live their best life by encouraging personal growth and self-awareness.

Faisal's writing style is both entertaining and approachable, appealing to a wide range of readers. His words inspire, encourage, and instill a feeling of purpose in readers. His leadership encourages individuals to embrace their passions, grow resilience, and create a life that resonates with their beliefs and objectives.

Faisal's devotion to personal progress and sharing optimism is evident in his interactions with readers, as well as his written works. He exemplifies humility and sensitivity, constantly attempting to connect on a deeper level with his audience. His sincere desire to create a positive influence seeps through his works, establishing him as an author who truly cares about his readers' well-being.

Mohd Faisal's writings are inspirational beacons, providing significant insights and direction to individuals seeking personal and spiritual progress. He motivates others to embrace their unique journeys, bringing them to a life of fulfillment, purpose, and inner peace.

BOOKS BY THIS AUTHOR

Sunshine In Your Pocket: Embracing Life's Challenges With Active Optimism

Are you tired of life throwing lemons at you? Well, worry no more because "Sunshine in Your Pocket: Embracing Life's Challenges with Active Optimism" is here to save the day! This book is your best guide to beating hurdles with a big smile on your face and a skip in your step.

Imagine a world where problems are met with laughter instead of tears, where mistakes are viewed as stepping stones to success, and where positivity reigns supreme. That's exactly what this book claims to give. Packed with funny tales, familiar stories, and useful tips, it will turn you into the ultimate optimist.

Gone are the days of wallowing in self-pity and sinking in negativity. "Sunshine in Your Pocket" will teach you how to turn every problem into a chance for growth. From learning to dance in the rain to finding the silver lining in every cloud, this book is your secret tool to becoming a source of happiness.

But wait, there's more! Along with the fun and uplifting content, you'll find easy-to-follow workouts and inspiring quotes to keep you inspired on your journey to accepting life's obstacles. With every page turned, you'll feel a surge of energy and a fresh zest for life.

So, why wait? Grab a copy of "Sunshine in Your Pocket: Embracing Life's Challenges with Active Optimism" and start on the journey of a lifetime. Say goodbye to gloom and doom and say yes to a life filled with joy, courage, and endless potential. Get ready to shine bright like the sun, my friend!

How To Deal With A Narcissist: Escaping The Grip Of Narcissistic Control

Are you tired of a narcissist in your life manipulating, controlling, and draining you emotionally? If so, "How to Deal with a Narcissist: Escaping the Grip of Narcissistic Control" is the book for you. This powerful book will teach you practical ideas and procedures for breaking out from the destructive cycle and regaining control of your life.

You'll discover how to navigate the intricate realm of narcissism and comprehend the fundamental mechanics of their conduct in this book. You'll learn about the many sorts of narcissists and their strategies, getting vital insight into how they function. You will be able to spot their manipulative ways and defend yourself from their influence with this information.

However, what distinguishes this book is its unique method - employing their own techniques against them. The author presents practical tactics and psychological insights to outwit and disarm narcissists based on considerable study and real-life experiences. You may reclaim your control and express your limits by knowing their weaknesses and manipulating their desire for adoration.

Inside "How to Deal with a Narcissist," you'll find:
Extensive descriptions of narcissistic personality characteristics and actions, assisting you in identifying narcissists in your life. Strategies for regaining your autonomy and self-worth by dismantling their influence and establishing healthy boundaries.

Techniques for navigating conflict and protecting your emotional well-being.
Ways to strengthen your resilience and create a strong support network to help you overcome the effects of narcissistic abuse.
Insightful case studies and real-life examples show how to use the ideas in a variety of scenarios.
Self-care techniques for healing and rebuilding your self-esteem after coping with a narcissist.
This book, written in a straightforward and entertaining language, gives you the skills and information you need to reclaim control of your life. It gives you the ability to break free from the hold of narcissistic control and go on a path of healing, self-discovery, and personal progress.

If you're ready to break away from a narcissist's harmful influence, "How to Deal with A Narcissist: Escaping the Grip of Narcissistic Control" is the book for you. It's time to reclaim your power, rebuild your life, and look forward to a future full of self-love, honesty, and perseverance.

Last Minute Magic: Channeling Procrastination Into Success With No Efforts.

Are you tired of constantly putting things off until the last minute, only to feel stressed and overwhelmed when the deadline finally arrives? It's time to embrace your procrastination tendencies and turn them into a secret weapon for success! Introducing "Last Minute Magic: Channeling Procrastination into Success With No Efforts" - the ultimate guide to mastering the art of procrastination and using it to achieve your goals effortlessly.

In this book, you'll discover the secrets to harnessing the power of procrastination, including practical tips and strategies for effective time management, productivity hacks, and simple yet powerful mindset shifts that will help you break free from the cycle of procrastination and finally achieve your dreams. With "Last Minute Magic," you'll learn how to turn your procrastination into a superpower, harnessing its energy to fuel your success and transform your life.

Whether you're a chronic procrastinator or simply looking to boost your productivity and achieve your goals with ease, "Last Minute Magic" is the ultimate guide to channeling procrastination into success with no efforts. So what are you waiting for? Start reading now and discover the magic of procrastination!

39 Hidden Commandments: For Financial Success, Money Making And Stress-Free Life.

Are you tired of feeling stressed and unfulfilled in your life? Are you ready to take control of your finances and relationships? Look no further than "39 Hidden Commandments for Financial Success, Stress-Free Life, and Self-Actualization, Better Family and Social Relationships."

In this book, you'll discover practical, actionable advice to help you achieve your goals and live your best life. From creating a budget and building wealth to improving your communication skills and nurturing your relationships, these commandments will guide you every step of the way.

With witty and relatable anecdotes, this book will not only educate but also entertain and inspire you. You'll learn the importance of self-care, time management, and goal-setting, and how to apply these concepts to your own life.

So, whether you're a recent graduate just starting out or a seasoned professional looking to improve your life, "39 Hidden Commandments for Financial Success, Stress-Free Life" is the ultimate guide to achieving your dreams and living a fulfilling life.

The Ikigai Blueprint : The Secrets To Financial Freedom For A Rich And Fulfilling Life.

"The Ikigai Blueprint: For A Rich And Fulfilling Life" is a guidebook that delves into the Japanese concept of Ikigai and provides a roadmap for finding purpose and fulfillment in life.

Based on the teachings of the Japanese island of Okinawa, the book explores the four key elements of Ikigai - what you love, what you are good at, what the world needs, and what you can be paid for - and shows how these elements can be combined to create a fulfilling life.

The book combines practical advice, inspiring stories, and thought-provoking exercises to help readers find their own personal Ikigai and live a life filled with joy, purpose, and meaning. Whether you are seeking to improve your career, deepen your relationships, or simply live a more fulfilling life, "The Ikigai Blueprint" provides a blueprint for creating a life of abundance, happiness, and purpose.

THE END

THE END

www.ingramcontent.com/pod-product-compliance
Lightning Source LLC
Chambersburg PA
CBHW011403210526
45464CB00008B/3031